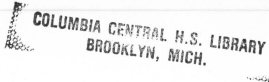

W9-CGV-151

WITCHES

OPPOSING VIEWPOINTS®

Look for these and other exciting *Great Mysteries:*

GREAT MYSTERIES

WITCHES

OPPOSING VIEWPOINTS®

by Bryna Stevens

Greenhaven Press, Inc.   San Diego, California

Book design by Joan Gordon, Minneapolis
Cover design by FAB Artists, Minneapolis
Cover illustration adapted from an illustration by Hans Weiditz, from Petrarca's *Von de Artzney Veider Gluck*, 1532

Library of Congress Cataloging-in-Publication Data

Stevens, Bryna.
    Witches : opposing viewpoints / Bryna Stevens.

       p.   cm. — (Great mysteries)
    Bibliography: p.
    Includes index.
    Summary: Examines several issues related to witches, including what happened in Salem and whether witches really fly, and incorporates the opposing views of experts.
    ISBN 0-89908-054-5 : $12.95
    1. Witchcraft—Juvenile literature.   [1. Witchcraft.]   I. Title.
II. Series: Great mysteries (Saint Paul, Minn.)
BF1566.S78 1988
133.4'3—dc19   87-18346
                                                                        CIP
                                                                             AC

Dedicated to women of mystery everywhere.

Contents

"When men and women lose the sense of mystery, life will prove to be a gray and dreary business, only with difficulty to be endured."
Harold T. Wilkins, author of Strange Mysteries of Time and Space

Introduction

"Penetrating so many secrets, we cease to believe in the unknowable. But there it sits nevertheless, calmly licking its chops."

H.L. Mencken, American essayist

This book is written for the curious—those who enjoy the hunt for possible solutions to the unexplained.

Mysteries are everywhere. To be human is to be constantly surrounded by wonderment. How do birds fly? Are ghosts real? How sophisticated is animal communication? How did the first baker discover how to make bread? Why are there no more dodo birds? Was King Arthur real or a fiction? Where did the world come from? Where is it going?

Great Mysteries: Opposing Viewpoints books are intended to offer the reader an opportunity to explore some of the many mysteries that both trouble and intrigue us. For the span of each book, we want the reader to feel that he or she *is* a scientist exploring the extinction of the dinosaur, an archaeologist exploring the origins of the great Egyptian pyramids, a psychic detective exploring the existence of magic.

One thing all mysteries have in common is that there is no ready answer. Often there are *many* answers but none on which even the majority of authorities agrees. *Great Mysteries: Opposing Viewpoints* books introduce the intriguing views of the experts, allowing the reader to participate in their explorations, their theories, and their disagreements as they try to explain the mysteries of our world.

But most readers won't want to stop here. *Great Mysteries: Opposing Viewpoints* aim to stimulate the reader's curiosity. Although truth is often impossible to discover, the search is fascinating. It is up to the reader to examine the evidence, to decide whether the answer is there—or to explore further.

One

Why Did People Condemn Witches to Death?

It's not hard to find witches with broomsticks on Halloween night. Perhaps you've dressed that way yourself or helped a friend prepare a fancy witch's costume. Perhaps you even found a black cat to accompany you, making the outfit seem spookier and more realistic.

Today, most people who dress up as witches on Halloween do it just for fun and no one is very much afraid of them. But people who lived a few hundred years ago didn't find anything funny about witches. No one who lived in fourteenth-century Europe or seventeenth-century America would have dared dress as a witch openly. To do so probably would have meant death. Many people thought that when something bad happened, it was because a witch had cast an evil spell. People, mainly women, were accused of casting such spells. Many of these accused were put to death by burning or hanging.

The case of Lydia Gilbert is typical of the way mid-seventeenth-century New Englanders blamed unfortunate events on witches.

Accident or Magic?

Henry Stiles, a bachelor, had found life lonely after his brother moved away from Windsor, Connecticut, so he invited Lydia Gilbert and her husband Thomas to move into his big farmhouse with him. Lydia cleaned house, cooked, and sewed for Henry as well as for her own family. They all lived together for three years until one day in November 1651 when Henry was shot by Thomas Allen.

Thomas Allen, a soldier, was participating in a military exercise. Suddenly his gun knocked against a tree. The gun fired. Henry Stiles, who played in the military band and happened to be nearby, was mortally wounded. A few weeks later the "particular court" found Thomas Allen guilty of "homicide by misadventure." For his "sinful neglect and careless carriages" he was fined twenty pounds and "bound to good behavior" for the following year with the provision "that he shall not bear arms for the same term."

But the matter did not end there. People wondered why this tragic event occurred. Were both men being punished by an angry God for past sins? Or was something evil at work?

Lingering Questions

The questions lingered on. Three years after the event, Jonathan Gilbert, a marshal, arrested his own mother. The indictment charged: "Lydia Gilbert, not having the fear of God before thine eyes, hast of late years or still dust give

——❝——

Of the witch-trial victims who were in fact witches, quite a number must have been genuinely guilty of the malice with which they were charged; malice begets malice, and terror, terror."

Author Stewart Farrar, What Witches Do

Entertainment to Satan, the great Enemy of God and mankind, and by his help hath killed the body of Henry Stiles, besides other witchcrafts for which according to the law of God and the established law of this commonwealth, thou Deservest to Dye."

In effect, the court asked, "Was Lydia Gilbert a witch? Did her witchcraft cause Thomas Allen's gun to discharge and kill Henry Stiles?"

Statements were taken from eyewitnesses and others. Several said that there was some anger between Lydia Gilbert and Henry Stiles. Also, she owed him money. The jury

This woodcut illustration of English witches being hanged comes from a law book published in 1678 in Scotland.

weighed the evidence and reached a verdict: "Guilty as charged." Her sentence was death by hanging.

The pastor of the Windsor Church agreed with the verdict. A few Sundays after the execution, he asked in a sermon, "Why has this terrible scourge of witchcraft been visited on our little community?

"The Windsor townfolk are themselves at least partly to blame," he said. "More and more, in recent months, they have strayed from the paths of virtue....In such circumstances the Devil always finds an opening; on such communities God

German witch-finder Konrad von Marburg passing sentence on a young woman.

brings retribution. Thus the recent witchcraft episode is a lesson to the people of Windsor to mend their ways."

Was the minister right? Had the devil "found an opening" in the little town of Windsor?

Why Did People Believe?

Lydia Gilbert was only one of many people put to death for practicing witchcraft. Why did people who lived then believe in witches and magic?

George Lyman Kittredge, in *Witchcraft in Old and New England*, states: "Our forefathers believed in witchcraft because they were men of their time. They shared the feelings and beliefs of the best hearts and wisest heads of the 17th century." In other words, it was probably more common to believe in witches than not to.

An Effort To Control Life

Psychologist Bronislaw Malinowski believes that early people's belief in magic came from the sense of despair they felt living in a world beyond their control. Primitive people, he says, looked to magical explanations when mysterious and terrible things happened. They believed, for example, that an evil person could use magic and cast a spell to cause a flood or famine.

> *" We intuitively understand that during the long centuries when women were the semislaves of society, they were naturally drawn to witchcraft as a cure for their powerlessness, a means of manipulating a world that otherwise painfully manipulated them."*
> *Author Erica Jong,* Witches

Magic gave people a feeling of control over their lives. If they believed other people used magic, they could understand *why* things happened. If they could use magic, they could *make* things happen.

Children often experience a sense of powerlessness. They live in a world ruled by adults. It might seem to them as though only magic can make their dreams come true. Only through magic can life's difficult problems be solved. Is this why children love stories about heroes who defy natural laws? Fairy godmothers, Superman, and Mighty Mouse don't have to obey the laws of science or of adults, yet they crush evil and cause good to triumph.

Records show that people in early cultures used magic to

try to bring about both good and bad deeds. In most cultures, it was only certain people who had the power to work magic. These people were known as magicians, sorcerers, wizards, warlocks, and witches.

Good magic, often called White Magic, was used to do good: to bring rain for dry crops, to prevent hailstorms, to make animals and crops grow and prosper, to gain true love, or to win a battle. Black Magic was used to do evil: to ruin an enemy's crops, to cause a neighbor's cows to sicken, or to prevent a rival from winning a contest. All cultures frowned on the use of Black Magic. Ancient Greece and Rome actually had laws forbidding it.

> " *Certainly I remember to have heard of far more cases of women than men: and it is not unreasonable that this scum of humanity should be chiefly drawn from the feminine sex...since that sex is the more susceptible to evil counsels.* "
> Author Nicholas Remy, Demonolotry, 1595

Have you ever crossed your fingers before you dared look at your report card or an exam grade? Did you ever own a rabbit's foot or search for a four-leaf clover, hoping it would bring you luck? If so, do you, too, believe in magic? Is Malinowski right? Is it a longing for control that makes people believe in magic?

Magic and Religion

Julio Caro Baroja, in *The World of Witches*, writes that magic and religion, especially in primitive cultures, are closely related. People used both magic and religion to fulfill their desires. Magicians and witches usually practiced magic to

During medieval times witches were thought to be able to control weather. These 15th-century witches are credited with making either rain or hail.

In making a magic charm, these witches are adding snakes and birds to a pot full of poisonous plants, animal organs, and human blood.

achieve their goals; priests usually prayed. But often magicians and priests did some of both.

Many people in early times looked upon the mysterious forces of nature as gods. When the sky god was angry, it expressed anger with thunder and bolts of lightning. Sometimes an angry god could be appeased with magic or with prayer. Sometimes it worked better to use both.

Gods in pre-Christian religions were both male and female. Caro Baroja states that in many of the early religions the sun god was male and the moon god female. During the day when

Collecting herbs and plants for healing.

> *The Science of Magick is not evil, for by the knowledge of it, evill may bee eschewed, and good means thereof may be followed."*
> Scholar and philospher Albertus Magnus,
> thirteenth century

the sun shone, life advanced. Crops were tended; animals were hunted for food. At night when the moon was out, life stood still. The world slept—except for those mysterious creatures that thrived in darkness. Thus, the female moon god became associated with mystery, darkness, and even death. In many cultures this sense of dark mystery transferred to mortal women. They possessed a unique power: They brought life into the world, something no man, not even a king, could do.

> ❝ *Since magic that is harmful to another is called witchcraft, for that reason witchcraft is the force and power of harming others in accordance with an expressed or tacit pact with a demon."*
> *Scholar Giovanni Alberghini, 1671*

As nurturers of the young, women learned to heal the sick. They collected herbs and plants and learned their magical secrets. By trial and error they discovered which ones healed and which ones were deadly. Women who were especially skillful at such things came to be known as witches. They were held in great respect and sometimes fear, for if they could heal by magic, couldn't they also use magic to cause harm?

Women known as witches have existed for centuries. Yet author Erica Jong writes that witches weren't viewed as *evil* persons until the time period when Christians tried to stamp out pagan religions.

Pagans and Christians

In many cultures, gods were thought to be both good and evil. They felt the same passions as people. But the later Christian concept included only one God who was good. Evil became associated with God's enemy Satan, or the devil. Magic and people who performed it were thought of as evil because they took over God's role. Instead of leaving things to

Trial of a German witch.

God, witches and magicians tried to bring about change through magic. Some even called upon the devil and his demons for help.

By the fourteenth century, Christianity had become the strongest religion in Europe. Earnest Christians viewed pagan religions as evil because they did not worship the one true God. Author Margaret Murray states that the pagan horned god Dianus fit the Christian image of the devil. In the eyes of the Church, the devil and pagan practices—including witchcraft—were united.

At first, penalties for the pagan practice of witchcraft were light. People who believed in witches' powers were said to be deluded or a little crazy. But beginning in the late 1400s and for a period of about 200 years, both Church and state took witchcraft more seriously. During this period the Church waged an open war against the devil and the practice of witchcraft. Why did the Church take such a strong stand? Some experts believe it was to protect its own power.

Clifford Lindsey Alderman, in *Witchcraft in America*, writes that in the twelfth century many of the poorer classes of people became unhappy with the Catholic Church of Rome, the only official Christian church at that time. People began forming their own religious groups. Alderman states that the Church became so alarmed that it struck back with the Inquisition. The Inquisition investigated and tried heretics, those who defied the accepted teachings of the Church. The purpose of the Inquisition was to eliminate enemies of the Church by questioning, torture, and sometimes death.

Not all heretics were witches. People were tried for any

> *To deny the possibility, nay, actual existence of witchcraft and sorcery is at once flatly to contradict the revealed word of God in various passages of both the Old and New Testament, and the thing itself is a truth to which every nation in the world has in its turn borne testimony.''*
>
> English writer on law Sir William Blackstone, eighteenth century

During the Inquisition two Dominican monks are burned for signing a pact with the devil.

kind of straying from the beliefs of the Church. But all witches were heretics; anyone suspected of being a witch could be seized by the officials of the Inquisition.

Witches were said to worship the devil. They were accused of seizing and killing unbaptized babies and making potions from their bodies. They were accused of causing the Black Death, a plague that ravaged Europe, killing about one-third of its population. They were accused of causing violent disturbances in weather patterns, causing crop failures and famine.

> *During many ages there were witches. The Bible said so. The Bible commanded that they should not be allowed to live. Therefore the Church. . .gathered up its halters, thumbscrews, and firebrands, and set about its holy work in earnest. . . .Then it was discovered that there was no such thing as witches, and never had been. One does not know whether to laugh or cry."*
>
> *Author Mark Twain,* Europe and Elsewhere, *nineteenth century*

This illustration comes from a picturebook for Swiss youth dated 1869. It depicts a witch being bound to the stake for burning.

Were any of these things true? Many religious leaders claimed that they were. Even after the Inquisition was over, witches were hated and feared by many. Protestant Martin Luther in the sixteenth century, declared, "I would have no pity on these witches. I would burn them all."

Many opposed witchcraft because they claimed the Bible spoke against it. After Goody Knapp was executed in New England for witchcraft in 1653, a neighbor said: "It was long before I could believe this poor woman was a witch, or that there were any witches, till the word of God convinced me, which saith, 'Thou shalt not suffer a witch to live.'"

But translating the Bible from its original ancient languages into more modern ones has caused many arguments about the true meaning of many Bible passages. For example, in the King James version, translated in the early 1600s, Exodus 22:18 states, "Thou shalt not suffer a witch to live." Yet Rossell Hope Robbins points out in the *Encyclopedia of Witchcraft and Demonology* that the original word for *witch* in this quotation is a word meaning *poisoner*. Henry Charles Lea, a historian, suggests that passages about witches in the Old Testament really referred to diviners—people who foretold the future. Neither *poisoner* nor *diviner* is quite the same concept as *witch*. Are witches really condemned by the Bible? Religious and language experts continue to disagree.

Harsh Punishment

Johann Weyer, a sixteenth-century physician, spoke out against common beliefs held at that time. He stated that the Bible mentions nothing about witches making a pact with the devil. He argued that one should not punish men and women for their opinions and heresies even if they confessed to making a pact with the devil. Such admissions, he claimed, were usually made by women who were feeble, senile, or deluded.

A few people during the witch craze charged that the methods used to investigate witchcraft were too uncertain to be grounds for death. But witches continued to be condemned. Reports vary, but thousands, and perhaps millions, of people in Europe were accused of practicing witchcraft and were put to death.

The witch craze affected colonial Americans, too, who were plagued by many questions concerning witches. Were people known as witches the cause of strange illnesses and deaths? Could witches cast evil spells? If so, how should they be punished? Puritan minister Cotton Mather believed he had the answers. He demanded that all witches be hunted down and destroyed. Was Cotton Mather right?

Two

What Happened in Salem?

Many Americans find the Salem witch trials of the late seventeenth century shocking. Why were nineteen people hanged as witches? Why was Giles Cory, who refused to testify, pressed to death with heavy stones? And why was a child, four-year-old Dorcas Good, chained in prison near her mother until her mother was hanged for practicing witchcraft?

People in seventeenth-century New England believed that a witch was a person who had made a pact with Satan and therefore had strange and terrible powers. Writer Bernice Kohn states that even educated New Englanders were certain that witches could make babies sicken and die, dry up a mother's milk, cause plagues of locusts, set fires, kill cattle, sheep, and crops, and call forth diseases and other similar misfortunes.

Cotton Mather, a minister, is generally credited with fanning the flames of witch hysteria that tore through Salem, Massachusetts. Why did a man of God show no mercy toward

the Reverend George Burroughs? Others wanted to spare his life after he correctly recited the Lord's Prayer on the gallows. But Robert Calef, who witnessed the event, claimed that Cotton Mather shouted to the crowd: "Let me remind you, that the Devil is never more himself than when he appears to be an angel of light. This man is not what he appears to be." As a result, states Calef, the Reverend Burroughs met his death.

Marion L. Starkey, in *The Devil in Massachusetts*, suggests that Cotton Mather was not being insensitive to a fellow minister. Mather had seen the effect of mob violence at Boston executions. He was anxious to prevent the same thing from happening in Salem. Starkey argues that Mather believed the clergyman had had a fair trial. When the crowd at Burrough's hanging began arguing among themselves, Mather thought it best to get the execution over and done with and let the crowd go home.

Chadwick Hansen, in *Witchcraft in Salem*, states: "Cotton Mather was anything but the wild-eyed fanatic of tradition. Throughout most of the proceedings [of the Salem witch trials] he was a model of restraint and caution, and at one point he went farther than any of his colleagues dared go in proposing a method to protect the innocent."

Cotton Mather was opposed to using torture to gain confessions and he was opposed to the admission of spectral evidence, commonly accepted at that time. (Spectral evidence was the claim that a spirit or apparition of a person did something, usually evil, while the actual living body of the person might be someplace else, such as at home sleeping.) Unless guilt was clearly proven at witch trials, Cotton Mather urged, the accused merely should be punished, not executed. Yet did Mather's fiery sermons and his willingness to punish those not clearly proven innocent keep the witch hunt going?

The Witch Hunt Begins

The Salem witch craze began in February 1692 at the home of the Reverend Samuel Parris. Reverend Parris recalled: "When the calamities first began, the affliction was several weeks before such hellish operations as witchcraft were suspected."

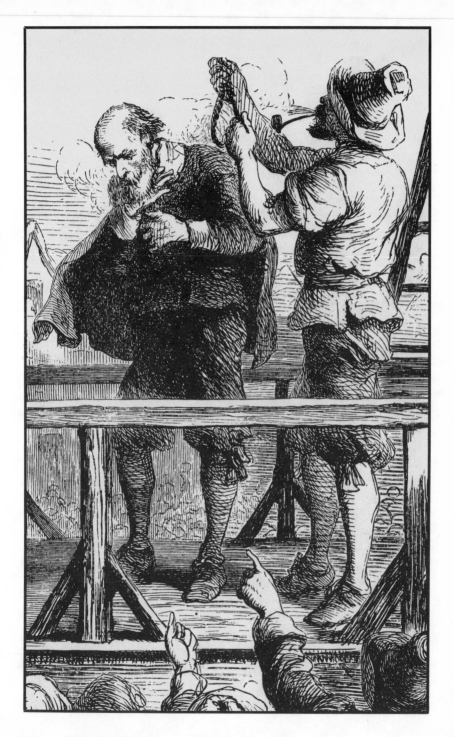

Men as well as women were accused of witchcraft.

Spectral evidence.

It was Tituba, the Parris family's slave, who eventually was blamed for much of the trouble. Tituba was born on the island of Barbados in the West Indies. Tituba knew a lot about casting spells and telling fortunes because witchcraft had been part of her life in Barbados.

Tituba's main job at the Parris's was to look after the family's nine-year-old daughter Betty and her eleven-year-old

> " *Were there no witches at all in Massachusetts in 1692? According to modern law there were none, none at least among the condemned.*"
>
> *Author Marion Starkey,* The Visionary Girls

cousin Abigail Williams, an orphan adopted by the family. Tituba entertained the girls with tales of voodoo magic that she'd learned in the West Indies. Soon other girls in the neighborhood began to stop by and listen. Anne Putnam, at twelve, was the youngest. Mary Warren, age twenty, was the oldest. Mercy Lewis, Susanna Sheldon, Mary Walcott, and Elizabeth Hubbard were teenagers.

The girls loved to look at Tituba's homemade crystal ball, made by dropping an egg white into a clear glass. Shapes seen in the egg white told the girls what their future husbands might be like. But the fun stopped when Anne Putnam claimed she saw a coffin.

Was Tituba's fortune-telling crystal predicting Anne's future?

Anne Putnam, an intelligent girl with an active imagination, had heard a lot about death and coffins from her mother. Her mother had lost many children. She often talked about her awful dreams in which her dead children reached out their arms to her piteously.

Today, psychologists say that children with dead siblings often feel guilty for being alive. Is that why Anne Putnam's behavior suddenly became so strange?

Anne began mumbling to herself, barking like a dog, and braying like a donkey. She scrambled under chairs and tables and made queer animal sounds. When she fell on the floor screaming and went into a convulsion, her father rushed to find Dr. Griggs, the town doctor.

Dr. Griggs wasn't surprised at Anne's behavior because recently he'd treated Betty Parris, Abigail Williams, Mary Walcott, and Susanna Sheldon for the same symptoms.

"The evil hand is on them," the doctor said.

Was Dr. Griggs right?

Rhoda Blumberg, in her book called *Witches*, states that

The Wonders of the Invisible World.

OBSERVATIONS

As well *Historical* as *Theological*, upon the NATURE, the NUMBER, and the OPERATIONS of the

DEVILS.

Accompany'd with,

I. Some Accounts of the Grievous Molestations, by DÆ-MONS and WITCHCRAFTS, which have lately annoy'd the Countrey; and the Trials of some eminent *Malefactors* Executed upon occasion thereof: with several Remarkable *Curiosities* therein occurring.

II. Some Counsils, Directing a due Improvement of the terrible things, lately done, by the Unusual & Amazing Range of EVIL SPIRITS, in Our Neighbourhood: & the methods to prevent the *Wrongs* which those *Evil Angels* may intend against all sorts of people among us. especially in Accusations of the Innocent.

III. Some Conjectures upon the great EVENTS, likely to befall, the WORLD in General, and NEW EN-GLAND in Particular; as also upon the Advances of the TIME, when we shall see BETTER DAYES.

IV. A short Narrative of a late Outrage committed by a knot of WITCHES in *Swedeland*, very much Resembling, and so far Explaining, *That* under which our parts of *America* have laboured!

V. THE DEVIL DISCOVERED: In a Brief Discourse upon those TEMPTATIONS, which are the more Ordinary *Devices* of the Wicked One.

By Cotton Mather.

Boston Printed by *Benj. Harris* for *Sam. Phillips*. 1693.

Two separate editions of a 1693 pamphlet written by Cotton Mather. The first,

The Wonders of the Invisible World:

Being an Account of the

TRYALS

OF

𝕾𝖊𝖛𝖊𝖗𝖆𝖑 𝖀𝖀𝖎𝖙𝖈𝖍𝖊𝖘,

Lately Excuted in

NEW-ENGLAND:

And of feveral remarkable. Curtofities therein Occurring.

Together with,

I. Obfervations upon the Nature, the Number, and the Operations of the Devils.

II. A fhort Narrative of a late outrage committed by a knot of Witches in *Swede-Land*, very much refembling, and fo far explaining, that under which *New-England* has laboured.

III. Some Councels directing a due Improvement of the Terrible things lately done by the unufual and amazing Range of *Evil-Spirits* in *New-England*.

IV. A brief Difcourfe upon thofe *Temptations* which are the more ordinary Devices of Satan.

By *COTTON MATHER*.

Publifhed by the Special Command of his EXCELLENCY the Goveneur of the Province of the *Maffachufetts-Bay* in *New-England.*

Printed firft, at *Bofton* in *New-England* ; and Reprinted at *London*, for *John Dunton*, at the *Raven* in the *Faudtry*. 1693.

printed in Boston, was then reprinted in London.

the girls were suffering from contagious hysteria, a mental illness caused by extreme fear, guilt, and stress. She observes that groups of people can "infect" one another and copy each other's symptoms.

At first Reverend Parris refused to accept the doctor's diagnosis. He tried curing the stricken girls through prayer and fasting, but that didn't work.

Word traveled fast in Salem village. Soon many people were wondering what to do about these children who at times appeared normal and at other times had strange fits. A few people thought the girls were faking their strange behavior just to get attention. They thought the girls should be punished. But most people in Salem agreed that the girls needed prayers a lot more than punishment.

> " Feeling their importance and not understanding how serious the matter was, [the girls] seem to have done some play-acting."
> *Author Alice Dickinson*, The Salem Witchcraft Delusion

Finally Reverend Parris called together some ministers from nearby towns and invited the girls and their families to join them. At first the girls sat quietly while the ministers prayed for them. But soon their fits began again. The girls screamed and yelled and threw themselves down on the floor as if in great pain. They made so much noise that the meeting broke up with no decision made about their strange sickness.

Tituba's Witch Cake

Mary Sibley, Mary Walcott's aunt, decided to take matters into her own hands. She paid a visit to Tituba since Tituba knew how to cast spells. Tituba baked a witch cake made from the girls' urine, mixed it with meal, and fed it to the Parris family dog, probably because she believed the dog was a familiar.

When Reverend Parris found out what had been done, he was furious. He said the witch cake was like going to the devil

Was Anne Putnam acting? Was she "infected" with contagious hysteria? Or had one of the Salem witches put a spell on her?

As this accused witch claims she is innocent, one of the "bewitched" girls

for help against the devil. "The Devil has been raised among us," he said, "and his rage is vehement and terrible; and when he shall be silenced, the Lord only knows." Reverend Parris chastised Mary Sibley in private and from the pulpit. Mary, in tears, said she was sorry.

But was it too late? Had the devil already been raised in Salem village?

Some people said the witch cake had worked. Hadn't the

falls to the floor in a fit.

girls at last told about their meetings with Tituba, and hadn't they named Sarah Good and Sarah Osborne as witches?

People had no trouble believing Sarah Good was a witch. Sarah smoked a pipe, was slovenly, and was a beggar. People had blamed her for a recent smallpox epidemic. Her four-year-old daughter Dorcas testified that her mother kept three birds, which the authorities decided were familiars. The afflicted girls displayed teeth marks on their arms that they said were

Thomas Satterwhite Noble painted "The Salem Martyr" in 1869. This young woman has been found guilty of practicing witchcraft and is walking with her judges and the hangman to the gallows.

caused by Dorcas's shape, or specter. Sarah Good denied she was a witch, but every time she looked at the girls they fell on the floor and had fits.

Sarah Osborne wasn't poor, but she had lived with her husband before marrying him, a fact that the people of Salem had neither forgotten nor forgiven. Also she hadn't attended a church meeting in more than fourteen months. She explained that she couldn't attend church because she was ill. But people in Salem thought there was something suspicious about her illness.

Whenever Sarah Osborne looked at the girls during her trial, they screamed and yelled and had fits.

Guilt and Innocence

Both Sarahs denied they were witches, but Tituba, after being beaten by Reverend Parris, admitted her guilt. "The devil came to me and bid me serve him," said Tituba.

Was Tituba telling the truth? Had the devil really paid her a visit? Most of the people of Salem believed that he had. Tituba was imprisoned but not executed.

When Giles Cory was accused of being a witch, he refused to testify. (His wife Martha had already been hanged for practicing witchcraft.) Without a plea, according to the law, Giles Cory couldn't be tried. But he could be subjected to painful punishment to force him to enter a plea. Heavy stones were placed on his chest. At first Giles Cory remained silent, but finally he let out a groan and died without testifying.

When Nehemiah Abbott came to trial, Mercy Lewis stood up and said he was not one of those who had been tormenting her. The other girls disagreed, and Nehemiah was searched for witchmarks. A witchmark is an unusual marking on the body such as a wart or birthmark. People believed a devil or familiar sucked the mark to gain nourishment. Since no witchmarks were found on Nehemiah, he was freed.

Nineteen people were hanged for practicing witchcraft during the Salem witch craze. Sarah Osborne died in prison before she could be hanged. More than 150 people were accused of practicing witchcraft and were arrested.

The lives of accused witches who confessed their guilt were spared. Those who refused to confess but were found

This 1892 illustration provides us with a typical Salem courtroom scene. Accusations almost fly through the air.

guilty in court were executed. Why did Salem authorities allow those who admitted their guilt to live? Clifford Lindsey Alderman, in *A Cauldron of Witches*, states that Salem officials hoped guilty witches who were shown mercy would reveal the names of other witches who hadn't yet been discovered.

The End of the Salem Witch Hunt

The Salem witch trials lasted from March to September 1692. Clifford Lindsey Alderman reports that the Salem witch trials ended when Governor Sir William Phips returned from a visit to Canada and discovered that his wife Mary had been accused of being a witch. He demanded that Chief Justice Stoughton stop the witch trials and release accused witches from prison.

The Chief Justice obeyed Governor Phip's order but stormed: "We were in a way to have cleared the land of them....The Lord be merciful to this country!"

66
I am falsely accused."

Sarah Good, accused and convicted of being a witch, 1692

Was Chief Justice Stoughton right? Was Governor Phips making a terrible mistake by ending the witch trials and freeing accused witches? Were the accused really guilty of doing wrong? Were they really witches?

Repentance

On December 23, 1696, Samuel Sewell, the presiding judge at the witch trials, sat in mourning because his two-year-old daughter had just died. He asked his son to console him by reading from the Bible. His son opened the Bible at random and read: "But if ye had known what this meaneth: 'I will have mercy and not sacrifice,' ye would not have condemned the guiltless."

The words "ye would not have condemned the guiltless" stuck in his mind. Is that what he had done, he wondered, condemned the guiltless?

> "*[Sarah Good's] answers were in a very wicked, spiteful manner, reflecting and retorting against the authority with base and abusive words and many lies. . . . It was said that her husband said that he was afraid that she was either a witch or would be one very quickly.*"
>
> A clerk at Sarah Good's trial, 1692

COTTON MATHER, D. D.

Born 12 Feb: 1663; died 13 Feb: 1728 A E. 65.-

Judge Sewell confessed before the entire congregation of his church that he had been wrong in his judgments of the accused witches. He did penance for the rest of his life. Other people who had participated in the witch trials also confessed that they had been wrong. Anne Putnam read her confession from the pulpit of Salem Village Church in 1706:

I desire to be humbled before God for that sad and humbling Providence that befell my father's family in the year about '92: that I, then being in my childhood, should by such a Providence of God be made an instrument for the accusing of several persons of a grievous crime, whereby their lives were taken from them, whom now I have just grounds and good reason to believe they were innocent persons. . . . I can truly and uprightly say before God and man, I did it not out of anger, malice or ill will to any person, for I had no such thing against any of them; but what I did was done ignorantly, being deluded by Satan.

In 1711 the Massachusetts General Court reversed its decision against the witches. Even Cotton Mather, who

"Last of the Old Witch Houses, Salem, Massachusetts, 1876."

continued to believe in witches, admitted to being plagued by guilt. He wrote in his diary that he should have used more vigor to stop the proceedings.

People in twentieth-century Massachusetts looked back on the Salem witch trials and decided they were a blot on the state's history. In 1957 the Commonwealth of Massachusetts freed all of the accused witches from blame.

Why?

Why did the Salem witch trials happen at all?

Chadwick Hansen, in *Witchcraft in Salem*, states that it's wrong to conclude that all people charged with practicing witchcraft in Salem were innocent. He writes that some of them were probably guilty. At the very least, practicing witchcraft was illegal in seventeenth-century Massachusetts Bay Colony.

Author George Lyman Kittredge disputes the idea that in 1692, New Englanders "should have known better." He finds it surprising that witchcraft outbursts didn't occur before. He states: "It is not strange there should have been witch trials. The wonderful thing is that they did not come sooner or last longer. More were put to death in a single county in England, in a short space of time, than have suffered in all New England from the first settlement to the present time. The frank public confession of error made by many [Salem] accusers is without parallel in the history of witchcraft."

Whether or not the witches of Salem deserved their persecution and punishment may still be debated by some. There's no question that people who were called witches frightened and offended many people in both America and Europe. What did they do that was so frightening? How did people determine who was a witch?

How Were Witches Detected?

How did people decide if someone was a witch?

During the Inquisition, in order to discover who were witches and who weren't, a judge came into an area and posted notices on public buildings. The notices asked people to identify others they suspected of practicing witchcraft. The notices said no one would be punished if found innocent. But in reality it was not only the guilty who were punished.

Guilty Until Proven Innocent

At that time accused witches were considered guilty until proven innocent. Witnesses were not allowed to testify on their behalf. Witnesses who testified against accused witches were not identified, so accused witches might never know who testified against them. They were not allowed to appeal their cases either. Having a good reputation and no history of ever

TRYALS
of Salem Witche

committing a crime were not taken into account. Usually accused witches weren't allowed to be defended by a lawyer either, because such a lawyer would then be guilty of defending heresy. Judges were encouraged to trick witches into confessing.

Among the questions accused witches were asked at their trails were:

How long have you been a witch?
Why did you become a witch?
What injury have you done to such and such person and how did you do it?
Who are the children on whom you have cast a spell?
What plagues of vermin and caterpillars have you created?

Didn't questions such as these assume guilt rather than protect the innocent?

People believed one sure way of discovering witches was to look for unnatural marks on their bodies—marks like warts, moles, birthmarks, or extra nipples or breasts. Most people believed that a witch's familiar suckled on these marks to gain

An apprentice sorcerer steps forward to receive a claw mark from Satan.

Celtic tradition held that witches in England had tattoos on their left hands—the hand used for sorcery.

nourishment. Such marks, wrote Michael Dalton in 1618, "Being pricked will not bleed, and be often in their secret parts and therefore require diligent search."

Several years ago author Margaret Murray conducted a survey of 315 people and discovered that seven percent had extra nipples and breasts on their bodies. And Thomas Ady, who lived in the seventeenth century, remarked: "Very few people in the world are without privy marks such as moles, stains, even such as witchmongers call the devil's privy marks and many an honest man or woman have growing on their bodies such as witchmongers call the devil's biggs [extra nipples]."

Some people said familiars sucked blood as well as milk from a witch's body. But Thomas Ady remarked that poor people needed all the blood they had. There would be none left over to give to familiars.

Witch finders claimed these marks were made by the devil with his talon or cloven hoof. They said the devil made such a seal to mark those with whom he'd made a pact. Great public displays were made of searching and shaving suspected

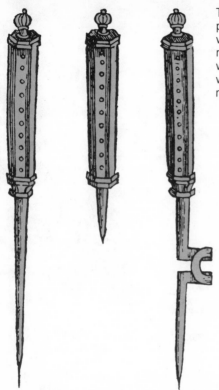

Three types of bodkin or pricker used to test witchmarks. The two straight needles were retractable and were used by unscrupulous witch finders to "prove" a mark was made by the devil.

witches to determine if "a devil's mark didn't lurk under the hair anyplace."

Did such a thing as a devil's mark exist?

Margaret F. O'Connell says that some witches in Britain followed Celtic traditions and had tattoos on their left hands, the hand used for sorcery. According to O'Connell, one coven (group) of witches claimed their chief had marked each of their fourth fingers by pricking between the upper and middle joints.

Bernice Kohn states that at a witch's initiation he or she was given a devil's mark. The mark was made by tattooing, forcing colored mud under the skin to form a raised area where the devil leader had bit or scratched with his claw.

Devil marks could be found anywhere on a witch's body, but common spots were shoulders, fingers, and hidden places such as the underside of an eyelid. Some devil marks were red; others were blue. Some were small and circular; others were made in the shape of animals such as dogs, toads, bats, or mice.

One version of the drowning test for witches.

Since witchmarks weren't supposed to bleed or cause pain, witch finders inserted a pin in a mark to discover if the mark had been made by the devil. Yet we know that pins carefully inserted under the skin or in a callus might not bleed or cause pain.

In England, Matthew Hopkins appointed himself as Witch-Finder General. Before that, he'd been a not-too-successful lawyer. Hopkins used an instrument known as a bodkin to detect witchmarks. But Hopkins's bodkin was no ordinary tool. When the instrument was pressed against an accused witch's body, its pin retracted into the handle so the accused didn't bleed or feel any pain.

Other Witch Tests

Another method Hopkins used to "discover" witches was the water test. The water test was based on a pre-Christian belief that water was sacred. Suspects were bound crosswise, right hand to left foot, left hand to right foot, and thrown into the water. It was believed that the accused person, if innocent, would sink. He or she would survive if rescued from drowning in time. If guilty, the suspects would float because the water had rejected them.

Suspected witches might also be tested by the scales test. Suspects were weighed against a metal-bound Bible on a huge set of scales. Accused witches were allowed to go free if they weighed more than the Bible.

Was this a fair test? A few who claimed it wasn't said weights could be hidden in a Bible to make the innocent appear guilty.

Accused witches might also be tortured. Rhoda Blumberg states that one reason torture was used was to get accused

A display of torture instruments used to force a confession from German witches in the 17th century.

witches to name others who were witches. One such person after being tortured named 150 other witches.

French demonologist Jean Bodin, who lived in the sixteenth century, defended the use of torture. He said: "If there is any way of appeasing the wrath of God, to gain his blessing, it is to punish witches with utmost vigor."

Others did not believe that torture brought about true confessions. Friedrich von Spee, a German scholar, wrote of forced confessions: "The most robust who have so suffered have told me that no crime can be imagined that they would

> " Contrary to popular belief, physical torture was not used to extract confessions. Testimony was taken on both sides, and character evidence favorable to the defendant was not uncommon. Guilt was never a foregone conclusion; indeed, many juries seemed reluctant to convict."
>
> *Author John Demos,* Entertaining Satan

An 1883 illustration titled, "Arresting a Witch."

not at once confess to, if it would bring a little relief, and then would welcome ten deaths to escape a repetition."

Johannes Junius of Bamberg, Germany, appears to have been an example of this. He was accused of practicing witchcraft. Shortly before he died he wrote to his daughter Veronica:

> Many hundred thousand good-nights, dearly beloved daughter, Veronica. Innocent I came into prison. Innocent I was tortured, innocent I must die. For whoever comes into witch prison must become a witch or be tortured until he invents something out of his head and, God pity him, thinks something up. And so I made my confession, but it was all a lie. I die innocent and a martyr.
>
> Good night for your father will never see you again.

The Judges

Some believe that the judges and other officials involved in witchcraft cases were cruel monsters without any trace of compassion, generosity, or pity. Others believe they were honest persons following their consciences.

Jeffrey Burton Russell, in *Witchcraft in the Middle Ages*, states: "The Inquisitors even argued, many of them with sincere conviction, that their persecution was a kindness, for by extracting confessions and repentance from the witches, by torture, if necessary, they might save their souls from the fires of hell even as their bodies were consumed by the fires of the stake."

Etienne Decambre, writing about witch trials in France, said most judges believed they were performing a religious service by pursuing the friends of the devil. They often used religious arguments to persuade witches to confess. "We have warned her to think carefully about herself and to have nothing on her conscience, for the good and salvation of her

---

" *The charges brought against the hundreds of women and men were senseless, and the trials themselves travesties of justice."*
Author Clifford Lindsey Alderman,
The Devil's Shadow

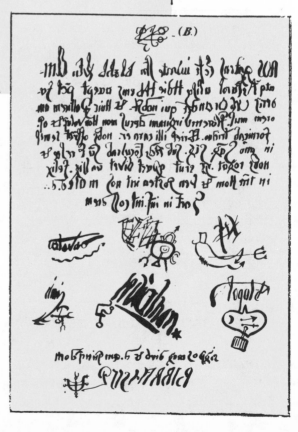

The pact between French priest Urbain Grandier and the Devil. It is supposed to be signed in Latin by none other than Lucifer and Satan.

Because the Inquisition judged that she was possessed by demons, this farm woman was hanged.

soul," said the judges of Amance. Witches were told that if they confessed, God would have mercy on them.

Many French peasants believed that witches who escaped death by denying they were allies of the devil would not receive pardon from God for their faults. And one self-confessed witch declared that witches who died without having made a confession in a court of law and receiving punishment, would go to hell.

Witch Hunts for Profit

A parish priest from a village near Bonn, Germany, wrote in the early 1600s: "Half the city must be implicated, for already professors, law students, pastors, canons, vicars, and monks have been arrested and burned. On the Eve of Our Lady's Day there was executed a young girl of nineteen who had the reputation of being the loveliest and most virtuous in all the city, and who from childhood had been brought up by the Prince-Bishop himself. To sum up, things are in such a

Witch trials provided income for many towns. Carpenters were paid to build gallows and innkeepers often sold refreshments at hangings.

> *It has never yet been known that an innocent person has been punished on suspicion of witchcraft, and there is no doubt that God will never permit such a thing to happen.*"
> Inquisitors Jakob Sprenger and Heinrich Kramer,
> Malleus Meleficarum, *1486*

Matthew Hopkins was a 17th-century English lawyer who made it his business to track down witches. Here he is depicted with two witches and their familiars.

pitiful state, that one does not know with what people one may talk and associate."

Discovering witches did not seem to wipe out the practice of witchcraft. Indeed, as more witches were discovered, more were accused. Perhaps the economy was one reason that persecution against witches continued. Persecuting witches was very profitable.

John Lindon, in *History of Treves*, notes that in Treves, France, a notorious witch-hunting state, witchcraft was a big business. He writes: "Notaries, copyists, and innkeepers grew rich. The executioner rode a blooded horse [a thoroughbred] like a noble in the court, and went dressed in gold and silver. His wife vied with noble dames in the richness of her array. The children of those convicted and punished were sent into exile. Their goods were confiscated."

Many people tried to bribe the inquisitors. Some people paid yearly fines. If they stopped paying, they were brought before the Inquisition again. The Inquisitors also got a percentage of the confiscated property. A witch was not allowed to die unless she confessed. Was this to save her soul, or was it because the money and property of a witch who died without pleading guilty went to her family, not the public treasury?

> 66 *Justice was perverted and thousands of innocent men and women died on the false evidence of envious or vengeful accusers."*
> Author Ronald Seth, Witches and Their Craft

Margaret F. O'Connell observes that by the sixteenth century, witch trials had turned into big business. If they had been stopped, the result would have been economic depression in many towns. The Inquisition employed judges, jailers, torturers, exorcists (those who cast out demons), wood choppers to provide wood for pyres on which to burn convicted witches, carpenters to build scaffoldings for hangings, messengers, notaries, scribes, and various other experts. Each received a fee. Doctors were paid to examine witches for devil's marks. Printers were hired to publish

Was Matthew Hopkins finally subjected to the same kind of drowning test that was used on the people he identified as witches?

notices against witches and to print books that supplied judges with the latest information about witches. Innkeepers and tavern owners sold refreshments to crowds that gathered to witness executions. They also catered banquets for the members of the court after every session.

Matthew Hopkins was well paid for witch-finding services. At a time when an average daily wage was sixpence, Hopkins received the equivalent of forty sixpence and more for discovering a witch. During their careers, witch finders Hopkins and his assistants earned over 1,000 pounds, equal to about 60,000 to 100,000 British pounds sterling (or 100,000 to 150,000 American dollars) today. Hopkins was responsible for the deaths of more than two hundred witches.

Eventually public feeling turned against Hopkins. Olga Hoyt says that he was seized, put to the swimming test, found guilty, and hanged as a wizard. But Rossell Hope Robbins says that Hopkins retired in 1646 and within a year died of tuberculosis. (Some people claim he got tuberculosis from the swimming test.)

Were profit and religion the only reasons that the witch craze continued as long as it did?

Jeffrey Burton Russell states that the Inquisition and secular and church courts cannot be blamed entirely for the cruelties against accused witches. Crowds that witnessed the persecutions, lynchings of witches by angry mobs, and the total lack of resistance in intellectual circles prove there was widespread support for the persecution of witches. He states that witch hunters could not have conducted public executions over centuries and throughout wide territories without the support or at least the quiet approval of the public.

"Witchcraft," says Russell, "springs out of the hostility and violence that are at the same time as old as man and as contemporary."

Four

Did Witches Really Fly?

The witch, dressed in black and screaming through space on her broomstick, is a popular figure at Halloween time. And who could forget the wicked witch in *The Wizard of Oz?* But did witches really fly?

Margaret Alice Murray, in *God of the Witches*, states that before the sixteenth century, reports of flights by witches were rare. But Erica Jong writes that *all* cultures had beliefs that witches could fly. She says that both Africans and Europeans believed that witches flew to their meetings by moonlight. Montague Summers also observes that the belief that witches could fly was universal. He writes: "Mid hurricane and tempest, in the very heart of the dark storm, the convoy of witches, straddling their broomsticks, sped swiftly along to the sabbat, their yells and hideous laughter sounding louder than the crash of the elements and mingling in fearsome discord with the frantic pipe of the gale."

> *Who is there that is not led out of himself in dreams and nocturnal visions, and sees much when sleeping which he has never seen while awake?"*
>
> The Canon Episcopi, *tenth century*

''A Witches' Frolick''

Author Jeffrey Burton Russell believes that the idea that witches could fly began in the traditions of the people of the Near East. He says this belief was reinforced by the Christian idea that demons, cast down from heaven, could remain in the air until the day of judgment.

Bernice Kohn, in *Out of the Cauldron*, states that our concept of a witch's behavior is a mixture of fact and fantasy. Is it only a fantasy to believe that witches can fly?

A Scottish Witch

Isobel Gowdie, an accused witch, claimed that she could fly. At her trial in Scotland in 1662, she declared:

> We take our windle-straws or beanstalks and put them between our feet and say thrice, 'Horse and hattock, Horse and pellatis, ho ho!' and immediately we fly to wherever we would. We fly like straws when we please. If anyone sees our straws in a whirlwind and does not bless himself, we may shoot him dead at our pleasure.

Was Isobel Gowdie telling the truth? Isobel willingly answered all questions put to her, without threats or torture. She made so many fantastic claims during her six-week trial that many said her words were simply the ravings of an insane woman and shouldn't be taken seriously.

> " *All the coven did fly like cats, jackdaws, hares and rooks.*"
>
> From a confession of Isobel Gowdie, 1662

There is no record of Isobel after her trial. She wasn't imprisoned or put to death for her crimes. Nancy Garden, in *Witches*, suggests that perhaps Isobel Gowdie was not a real person. Perhaps she was created by Scottish authorities to warn people about the horrors of witchcraft.

Montague Summers, the author of *The History of Witchcraft and Demonology*, states that although the witch is credited with the power to fly, there were very few confessions by witches who claimed to do so. But Isobel Gowdie was not the only witch who claimed she could fly.

In Salem, a woman named Foster confessed that the devil carried her and another woman through the air on a pole to a witch meeting. Unfortunately, the pole broke during the journey and they fell to the ground, injured. Tituba of Salem also confessed that she had flown to witches' sabbats (meetings) in the company of a tall man, a hog, two cats, and a familiar. "I was going and then came back again," said Tituba. "I never saw Boston. I never went to any town. I saw no trees, no town."

A man in Germany said he discovered that hitching a ride with a witch was dangerous. He said he once begged a witch to let him ride with her to a sabbat. The witch agreed. But when they were almost there he became frightened, changed his mind, and began praying. Suddenly he fell to earth. When he stood up, he discovered he was in a strange land. He said it took him three years of wandering before he was able to find his way back home.

Were these people telling the truth? Did they really fly as they claimed? Or is there a more ordinary explanation?

The term *flying* even today is often used in a general sense for moving quickly. We might say, "When the knock came, she flew to the door," or, "He flew around the room, straightening

books and cushions." Did witches
really only move quickly rather than
fly through the air?

Or might the idea of flying have
come from the sticks that commonly
were used by walkers to pole-vault
across the ground and across streams
to speed up a trip? Perhaps this gave
the impression to others that the
witches were flying.

In 1665 Julian Cox said that one
evening while walking near her home
she saw three persons carried up in
the air about a yard and a half from
the ground. Since witches leaped very
high during their dances, was it this
that Julian Cox saw?

Why did people believe witches
flew on broomsticks?

Once, the broom itself was thought
to be magical. This belief dates from
the time when trees were believed to
be magical. A fairy's wand was
probably a branch from a tree.

The first brooms were made from
the stalk of a broom plant with some
leaves at the end. The broom, an
indoor tool, became a symbol for
women who worked inside caring for
a home and children. Women in
England placed a broom in a chimney
so that it could be seen from the
outside. This told people that the
woman of the house was at home. A
broom placed outside the front door
meant a wife was absent and her
husband was free to entertain his
male friends without interference from
her.

Isobel Gowdie told the court that before leaving to attend a sabbat she placed a broom on her bed to represent herself to her husband and then said, "I lay this besom [broom] in the Devil's name; let it not stir till I come again."

Erica Jong reports that witches turned the broom, a tool of drudgery, into a tool of freedom and flight.

Flight or Fantasy?

A common question at the time of European witch trials was whether witches actually flew to the sabbat or only thought they did.

Jakob Sprenger, who said he believed sorcerers could be bodily transported, cited a case of a woman who confessed that she attended a sabbat every night. The woman said that neither bolts nor bars could prevent her from flying to those infernal revels.

The woman was put under lock and key in a chamber from which it was impossible to escape. She was observed closely by the guards. The guards reported that as soon as the door was closed she threw herself on the bed and became completely rigid. Doctors and select members of a tribunal entered the room. They shook her, gently at first, and then roughly. She was pulled and pinched sharply, but she remained still.

At last a lighted candle was brought in and placed against her

Animals were supposed to be a common conveyance to Sabbat.

naked foot until her flesh was scorched. The woman remained motionless as stone. When she awoke she sat up and related in detail the happenings at a sabbat she claimed she'd attended. She gave the place, the number in the witches' company, the rites, what was spoken, and what was done. Then she complained that her foot hurt.

Priests told her what had occurred and how she had never stirred from her bed. They told her that her sore foot was from a lighted candle they'd used in the experiment. The woman was given a suitable penance and then sent home.

What was the explanation for what happened? Had the woman greased herself with a drug-filled ointment? Was the woman mentally ill? Why did she believe she'd attended a sabbat when reliable witnesses declared she'd been in a deep sleep?

Flying Ointment

Ronald Seth, in *Witches and Their Craft*, writes, "Some later demonologists believed that witches did actually fly through the air astride broomsticks or on the backs of animals, but the earlier ones were skeptical and argued that the ointment was concocted of certain drugs which caused the hallucination of flying."

> **❝** *Certain women, converted to Satan, believe and confess that in the night hours they ride with Diana the goddess of the pagans....But you are crassly stupid to believe that these acts, which are imaginative, actually occur.*"
>
> *From a twelfth-century tract*

Traditional belief is that on the night of a sabbat a witch took off her clothes, greased herself and her broomstick with oil, and flew to the meeting.

Not all witches anointed themselves in oil, but many did. Swedish witches said that Antecessor, their god, "gives us a horn with salve on it, wherewith we anoint ourselves, whereupon we call the Devil and away we go."

The devilish connection was noted by Martin del Rio, a

Jesuit priest writing in 1599. He explained why he believed the ointment was used:

> The Demon is able to convey the witches to the sabbat without the use of any unguent, and often does so. But for several reasons he prefers that they should anoint themselves. Sometimes when the witches seem afraid, it serves to encourage them. When they are young and tender they will thus be better able to bear the hateful embrace of Satan who has assumed the shape of a man.

Erica Jong says the oils witches used to grease themselves contained powerful hallucinogens (drugs that cause hallucinations) powerful enough to kill a person in large doses. These drugs may have been absorbed through the skin and mucous membranes and entered a witch's bloodstream.

> " *Francoise Secretain said that, to go to the Sabbat, she placed a white wand between her legs and uttered certain words, and that she was then conveyed through the air."*
>
> French witch inquisitor M. Boguet

A.J. Clark states that one of the drugs witches commonly used produces mental confusion, dizziness, and shortness of breath. He claims another ingredient in the oils can make a person delirious. A third substance produces excitement and irregular action of the heart. Clark writes: "I cannot say whether any of these drugs would produce the impression of flying. [But] irregular action of the heart in a person falling asleep produces the well-known sensation of suddenly falling through space, and it seems quite possible that the combination of these drugs might produce the sensation of flying."

The Stick or the Rider

In early times just the stick was greased, but later the rider herself was anointed. Margaret Murray states, "It seems immaterial whether the stick or the rider were anointed;

All these plants are members of the Solanaceae family of herbs and shrubs. The climbing and creeping plants have been used medicinally since ancient times as stimulants, narcotics, pain relievers, and poisons.

Mandrake

This root is famous for its resemblance to the human form. It has been used since the Middle Ages as a painkiller. The superstitious claimed it brought wealth, love and children.

Henbane

The plant closely resembles a potato plant because they are members of the same family. The difference, of course, is that the potato is nutritious while the henbane plant has sticky, hairy leaves which produce a strong narcotic and poison.

Deadly Nightshade

Belladonna is its other name, Italian for beautiful lady. Women used to mix it with water and dilate their pupils. It is a poison and a sedative, used in Medieval Europe as an hallucinogen.

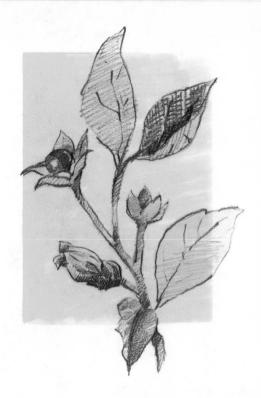

Thornapple

Some varieties are herbs, some are bushes or trees. Although the whole plant contains dangerous chemicals, the flowers had a reputation for being so narcotic that their scent alone could be dizzying or highly toxic.

Witches did anoint themselves with a salve, containing what we now call psychedelic drugs. . . . In the ecstasy of their dances, or merely on the way to them, but already under the spell of the drug, they imagined themselves flying through the air."

Author Hans Holzer, The Truth About Witchcraft

In this 16th-century engraving by Albrecht Dürer, a witch rides the devil's he-goat to a meeting.

sooner or later the sensation of flying would be felt and the rider would be convinced that she had flown through the air."

Harold A. Hansen, in *The Witch's Garden*, writes that today the witch's ride generally is not considered factual. He says that with the aid of drugged ointment, witches came into contact with a supernatural world, heard voices, saw phantoms, and afterwards could not understand that their experience had been a narcotic dream.

> **"** *There is no persuasive evidence for the existence of drug cults at the time of the trials. Although witches were often accused of using hallucinatory ointments, we can be certain that at least in some cases such charges were completely false."*
>
> Author Joseph Klaits, Servants of Satan

Is Hansen right? Were witches' confessions of flying based on their inability to separate their dreams from reality?

Since earliest times people dreamed of being able to fly like birds in the sky. Flying upward was associated with being good. Saints and others were rewarded by ascending to heaven. But, said those who hated them, witches flew at the devil's beckoning. They used their evil powers to fly to the sabbat.

Five

What Happened at a Witches' Sabbat?

"Of all the aspects of witchcraft," states Rossell Hope Robbins in the *Encyclopedia of Witchcraft and Demonology*, "the sabbat has attracted the most attention, both from the curious layman and the professional demonologist."

No one is certain of the exact derivation of the word *sabbat*. Some scholars believe *sabbat* evolved from the French word *s'esbattre*, which means "to frolic." Margaret O'Connell claims that the word *sabbat* is at least as old as the earth mother. She says that to the ancient Babylonians, *Sa-bat* meant "heart rest."

Nancy Garden offers a few other possibilities: *Sabazios*, an ancient god from Phrygia, in Asia Minor; *Sabaoth*, Greek, meaning "armies" or "hosts"; *Sabbatatious*, having to do with a feast.

Jeffrey Burton Russell, author of *Witchcraft in the Middle Ages*, states that the simplest answer is that *sabbat* is derived

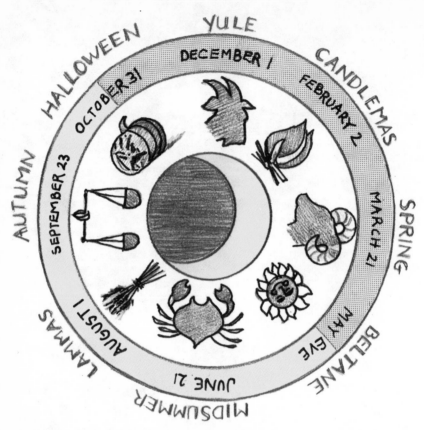

A circle is often used in witch ceremonies to symbolize the cycle of life. This circular calender is divided into the eight times of year commonly celebrated by witches.

from the Hebrew *shabbat*, the day of rest. Sometimes Christians of the Middle Ages referred to the sabbat as a synagogue. *Synagogue* is a Hebrew term that means "a gathering" or "place of worship."

Traditionally it is believed that witches' covens met about once a week or whenever members decided to get together, and there was always a gathering when the moon was full. Several times a year, different covens got together for a gala meeting. These were known as sabbats.

Margaret A. Murray states that when people think of witches' meetings, most think *only* of sabbats. But witches actually held two types of meetings—the esbat and the sabbat. Esbats were small meetings that were held weekly, usually at night. Sabbats, much larger gatherings, were held quarterly on the second of February, the Eve of May (April 30), the first of August, and the Eve of November (October 31). Murray says that these dates help prove that the witch cult was very old. These dates don't relate to agriculture or the equinoxes (the longest and shortest days of the year) but to the hunting and breeding of animals.

Rhoda Blumberg disagrees. "Margaret Murray's beliefs are not accepted by scholars today. There isn't any proof that witches were ever organized in the past," she writes.

A French Sabbat

Most of our ideas about what took place at a sabbat are based on witches' confessions at their trials. Much of this testimony was given as the result of threat or torture.

The trials of Anne Marie de Georgel and Catherine Delort

While a young man peeks in the window, a group of witches prepares to attend the sabbat. The notion that witches flew out through the chimney may have originated in ancient times when homes were underground and one had to exit through a hole in the roof.

Did some witches really dig up buried bodies in order to get ingredients for ointments? This 18th-century engraving, done by Jacques Aliamet, is called simply, "The Witches' Sabbath."

in 1335 in Toulouse, France, have always been of great interest to historians. It was at these trials that the word *sabbat* was used for the first time. At her trial, Catherine Delort said that at the sabbat she and other witches devoured the bodies of young children.

Anne Marie de Georgel claimed to have been a witch for twenty years. She said a man with black skin who had eyes that burned like coals and who wore animal hides had blown into her mouth and had given her the power to fly to a sabbat whenever she chose. Once there, she said, a he-goat taught her all kinds of secret spells. She claimed the he-goat explained poisonous plants to her and how to make different types of poisonous ointments. She said she got the ingredients by digging up bodies in cemeteries and by going to the gallows to obtain clothing, hair, nails, and fat from the bodies of dead criminals.

> *The women industriously concocted poisons and ointments out of black bread and the rendered fat of murdered infants. Having built up an appetite, they next banqueted on babies' limbs and toads."*
>
> Judge Pierre de Lancre, seventeenth century

Anne Marie said that God and the devil were equal; God ruled in heaven and the devil on earth. She said that God and the devil would struggle for all eternity, but at this time the devil was more powerful. She said she hoped to share in the devil's triumph. Is it any wonder then that religious people, on hearing such testimony, found witches and the power of the devil so frightening?

Anne Marie later begged to be forgiven for her sins and asked to be reconciled to the Church. Her pleas were ignored. Both she and Catherine Delort were burned at the stake.

Satan on his throne addressing witches and warlocks gathered for the sabbat.

Dancing with the Devil to music on the sabbat. Dated 1608, both these woodcuts are from Francesco Maria Guazzo's *Compendium Maleficarum*.

Olga Hoyt, the author of *Witches*, summarizes the events at a sabbat from reported confessions: After the witches convened for the sabbat, roll was called and new witches were introduced. Then witches reported their deviltry and made vows to continue dedicating their souls to the devil. Witches might be asked to kiss the devil, who appeared in a frightening disguise. Then the dancing began. This might be

> " *Descriptions [of sabbats]. . . were full of gory details. . . . To people in those days the sabbat was as real as it was grim. But in modern times it seems so improbable that some scholars have actually wondered if at least some of the details were invented by the Inquisition."*
>
> *Author Nancy Garden,* Witches

folk dancing done with clothes on or perhaps wilder dancing done naked except for masks. Some dancing was done in follow-the-leader style with an end man who whipped those who lagged behind.

Food and drink were served. Some witches confessed that at times the drink was blood; at other times it was black moss-water. The food might be "beefe, bacon, and roasted mutton." The witches, filled with drugs and wine, ate and drank in an atmosphere of frenzied enjoyment until cockcrow when the festivities ended. Hoyt adds, "It is easy to

understand why Christians considered the witches' Sabbats demonic exhibitions."

Margaret Murray traces the sabbat back to the pre-Christian era, even as far back as the Stone Age, but author Ronald Seth, in *Witches and Their Craft*, states that it was church leaders who thought up the sabbat. Witches then adopted the practice. He says the form the sabbat took was reported to follow almost exactly the form set up by Church authorities.

Did the kinds of activities described actually take place at

sabbats as the women reported?

In 1761 Dom Augustin Calmet, a French priest, stated: "To attempt to give a description of the Sabbat is to attempt a description of what does not exist and what has never existed save in the fantastic and disordered imagination of warlocks and witches. The pictures which have been drawn of these assemblies are merely the fantasy of those who dreamed they had actually been borne, body and soul, through the air to the Sabbat."

To which Henri Boguet, a seventeenth-century judge, responded: "Happy skeptic! But unfortunately the Sabbat did—and does—take place; formerly in deserted wasteland, on the hill-side, in secluded spots, now, as often as not, in the privacy of vaults and cellars, and in those lone empty houses innocently placarded 'To Be Sold.'"

Sabbat Descriptions Invented

Author Rhoda Blumberg, in *Devils and Demons*, states that "there is not the slightest proof that sabbats ever took place. Descriptions of sabbat celebrations came from confessions of frightened, deranged, and tortured people."

Many others familiar with the history of witchcraft agree that it was fearful circumstances such as the Inquisition in Europe that inspired accused witches to make up lurid tales of sabbat activities. Telling those tales was one way of protecting themselves from painful punishment.

In her book *Witches*, Nancy Garden maintains that sabbats were rarely mentioned in countries in which the Inquisition didn't operate, such as England. It wasn't until 1612 that a sabbat in England was reported.

Rossell Robbins agrees: "The conception of the sabbat seems to have been fabricated during the 14th and 15th centuries largely by the investigators and judges connected with the Inquisition." He claims that to early demonologists the sabbat was unknown. Yet by the sixteenth century the sabbat was an established part of witchcraft.

"For centuries," writes Olga Hoyt, "the Sabbats were gossiped about as being fantastic, horrible, drunken wild orgies. Perhaps they were some of that. But the witches. . .were excited, stimulated worshippers of a cult they

Satan is often depicted as a horned god. The witches dancing around him have curious demons for partners.

Feasting by moonlight.

believed in. There are various viewpoints as to what is possibly believable about these Sabbats, and what could only be the results of frightened, tortured imaginations of those testifying under pressure at trials. But as the savage tribal festivals among primitive people are real, it is conceivable that the Sabbats did occur as described."

Feasting

Feasting was an important part of the sabbat. Nicholas Remy, a French judge who bragged that he'd sentenced nine hundred witches to death in a fifteen-year period, described the food served there:

"All who have eaten at the Devil's table state that his dinners are both so disgusting to look at or stink so that the hungriest feels sick." De Lancre, another French judge, claimed that at a sabbat guests were served "no other meat but carrion [dead and putrefying flesh], and the flesh of those who had been hanged, and the hearts of children not baptized, and unclean animals strange to the custom and usage of Christian people, the whole savourless and without salt."

Not everyone agreed that the food at a sabbat was terrible. A London pamphlet of 1673 read: "They sit to Table where no delicate meats are wanting to gratifie their Appetites, all danties being brought in a twinckling of an Eye."

> " The meal, whether perceived by the eyes or by the sense of smell, produces nausea. The taste of the food itself is so unpleasant and tart and bitter that it has to be vomited out as soon as tasted."
>
> Author Nicholas Remy, Demonolotry, 1595

It was the joyousness of the witch cult that was particularly apparent during their feasts, Margaret Murray reports. She states that the feasts symbolized to the witches the gifts of God to people. When the weather was nice, the food was eaten in the open air. She claims the witches of Somerset, England, reported that "all sate down, a white Cloth being

He had eyes that burned like coals, hairy limbs with huge claws on hands and feet, and he carried a book with his followers' names scratched in.

spread on the ground, and did drink Wine, and eat Cakes and Meat."

Georgess McHargue states in *Meet the Witches* that the central feature of the sabbat was feasting and dancing. She explains that people in primitive cultures often viewed feasting and dancing as a magical way of making sure that the days to come would be filled with abundance and happiness.

Meet the Devil

Isobel Gowdie confessed that after they finished eating the witches looked steadfastly at the devil, bowed to him, and thanked him for the feast. Bernice Kohn states that the appearance of the devil or his representative was the highlight of the sabbat. She says that this creature might appear in an animal mask, tail, and horns, or a similar outfit.

It was also the devil's part in the sabbat that was most controversial, according to Nancy Garden, especially in places where the Inquisition was strong. She reports that not even accused witches agreed whether the Grand Master at a sabbat was the devil himself or someone dressed to look like him.

Agnes Simpson, at her witch trial in 1591, described a devil she saw at a sabbat: "The Devil appeared in the pulpit like a little black man, having a black book in his hand from which he called out the name of every one of them. Those who came close to him said his body was hard like iron. His face was terrible, his nose like the beak of an eagle, great burning eyes. His arms and legs were hairy with huge claws upon his hands and feet."

In contrast to the many horrible descriptions of sabbats, Margaret Murray reports that when Inquisitor de Lancre questioned a young witch, she told him that the sabbat was "true paradise where there was more joy than could be expressed." Murray states that the ceremonies celebrated by these witches had an air of gaiety and happiness that even the records made by Christian witch hunters and judges couldn't disguise completely.

Were witch sabbats joyful, even innocent, celebrations of nature? Were they horrible occasions highlighted by devil worship and sacrifice of animal and human victims? The reports that have passed down through the centuries about witches and their rituals offer conflicting testimony. The only real agreement is that witches remain a fascinating mystery.

What Happened to the Witches?

The witch craze ended in the eighteenth century, a century that became known as the Age of Enlightenment. Some say that the great minds and writers stopped believing in magic and miracles. Some people rejected belief in God and the devil. Those who continued to believe claimed that the universe was run by the laws of God and that these laws could be discovered through science. Nature's mysteries could be explained. Miracles and magic were natural things that were mysterious only because people had not yet been able to understand the rules that governed them. People of the eighteenth century believed in a rational explanation for everything.

In the nineteenth and twentieth centuries, witchcraft, to most people, seemed merely a curiosity. In 1951, Delaware removed an old law that threatened punishment to anyone practicing witchcraft, sorcery, enchantment, and conjuration. A

similar action was carried out in Great Britain in the same year.

But has witchcraft—and fear of it—died out?

Sybil Leek, an Englishwoman born in the 1920s, is one of the best known modern witches. She has written several books, including *Diary of a Witch*, and has been on numerous television talk shows. According to her, witchcraft is very much alive today. It is a religion and a science that happens to be one step ahead of conventional science. Leek and many others who claim to be witches believe that magic has rules and explanations—but we haven't figured them out yet. These people also believe that witches must use their magic for good purposes, to enhance life.

Others agree that witches are thriving in the modern world but believe that their influence is evil. In fact, in 1985 a prominent United States senator was influenced by worried and frightened voters to try to pass a law against the practice of witchcraft. And only a few years ago in Hungary, an old gypsy woman was burned at the stake for supposedly casting an evil spell on farm animals.

Do witches really exist? Halloween, a holiday observed mainly for fun, proves that witchcraft still excites our imaginations. And, although most people no longer believe that individuals known as witches possess magical powers, the practice of witchcraft has never died out. Perhaps it never will.

Books for Further
Exploration

Bryna Stevens recommends the following books:

Clifford Lindsey Alderman, *A Cauldron of Witches*. New York: Julian Messner, 1971.

Thomas G. Aylesworth, *Servants of the Devil*. Reading, MA: Addison-Wesley, 1970.

Rhoda Blumberg, *Witches*. New York: Franklin Watts, 1979.

Rhoda Blumberg, *Devils and Demons*. New York: Franklin Watts, 1982.

Alice Dickinson, *The Salem Witchcraft Delusion: 1692—"Have You Made No Contact with the Devil?"* New York: Franklin Watts, 1974.

Nancy Garden, *Witches*. New York: J.B. Lippincott Co., 1975.

Roger Hart, *Witchcraft*. New York: G.P. Putnam, 1972.

James Haskins, *Witchcraft, Mysticism, & Magic in the Black World*. New York: Doubleday, 1974.

Olga Hoyt, *Witches*. New York: Abelard-Schuman Ltd., 1969.

Bernice Kohn, *Out of the Cauldron: A Short History of Witchcraft*. New York: Holt, Rinehart, & Winston, 1972.

Georgess McHargue, *Meet the Witches*. New York: J.B. Lippincott, 1984.

Margaret F. O'Connell, *The Magic Cauldron: Witchcraft for Good and Evil*. New York: S.G. Phillips, 1975.

Frances Wilkins, *Wizards and Witches*. New York: Henry Z. Walck, Inc., 1965.

Selma R. Williams and Pamela J. Williams, *Riding the Nightmare: Women & Witchcraft*. New York: Atheneum, 1978.

Spells and Charms

Do witches really have magic powers?

Throughout this book, the author has referred to spells and charms witches were said to use. Although she has written about witches who lived centuries ago in the United States and Europe, belief in witches is worldwide. There are records of witches and witchcraft throughout human history in nearly every culture. In some societies, witches are accepted as a good influence; they are thought of as able to heal, to tell the future, and to help in finding fortune, love, and power. In other societies, they are condemned; they are considered to be evil and are thought to be working with the devil. But whether they are considered good or evil, they are known for the various kinds of spells and charms they use to do their work.

The words *spell* and *charm* are often used to mean the same thing—words or phrases that have a magical effect. *Abracadabra* is a traditional magical word or charm used in any number of spells. *Charm* also means an object which has magic powers. For example, in some cultures, a clove of garlic is thought to be a charm powerful enough to ward off the effect of an evil spell.

The rest of this appendix describes several spells and charms, some of which are traditional beliefs that don't mean a lot to us today; others are "magic" that you might want to try yourself.

Medical Charms

According to C.H. Wallace in *Witchcraft in the World Today*, the following charm was used in Italy *to cure a child of worms*. It was recited over the child once forward, once backward, a second time forward, and again backward.

> Holy Monday
> Holy Tuesday
> Holy Wednesday
> Maundy Thursday
> Good Friday
> Holy Saturday
> Easter Sunday
> Worms-on-the-run-day.

To get rid of warts, people in the southern United States would sometimes use this spell: First, split a bean. Then cut the wart with a knife and put one half of the bean on it so that the bean will absorb some of the blood or fluid that might come out. Burn the other half of the bean until there is not even an ash left. Then, on a midnight with no moon, take the half-bean that was on the wart to a crossroads and bury it, chanting, "Down bean, off wart, come no more to bother me."

Virginia Newall, in *The Encyclopedia of Witchcraft and Magic,* reports a charm used *to cure cramps.* Like many medieval charms, it combines belief in magic and in Christianity.

> There came three Angells out of the East
> The one brought fire, the other frost;
> In the name of the Father, and Son and Holy Ghost Amen.
> Cramp be thou faintless,
> As Our Lady was sinless,
> When she bare Jesus.

Another cure for cramps, according to Leonard R.N. Ashley in *The Wonderful World of Magic and Witchcraft,* is this charm:

> The Devil is tying a knot in my leg.
> Mark, Luke, and John, unloose it, I beg.
> Crosses three we make to ease us:
> Two for thieves and one for Jesus.

The *Kalevala,* an ancient Finnish epic, contained many spells. One of them, *to stop bleeding,* was:

> Listen, o blood, instead of flowing,
>   instead of pouring forth thy warm stream,
> Stop, o blood, like a wall,
> Stop like a hedge.
> Stop like a reef in the sea:
>   like stiff sedge in the moss,
>   like a boulder in the field,
>   like the pine in the wood.

In Mexico, a *limpia,* or cleansing, is the *cure for some sicknesses.* One kind of limpia includes the use of aromatic herbs such as laurel leaves. The leaves may be burnt and their pungent odor inhaled, or they may be steeped in boiling water to purify the air around the patient. The beard of a billy goat may also be passed over a flame, creating an odorous smoke that is inhaled to cleanse the patient inside. Throughout limpias, the witch and observers change and pray.

Often, according to C.H. Wallace, an egg is used in limpias. One ritual starts with drawing the sick person's face on the egg. Now the egg represents the patient, and the object of the limpia is to transfer the sickness from the patient to his or her representative, the egg.

To do this, the witch first sucks the patient in several places—

sucking until little blood specks appear. These suggest that the sickness or evil in the person is beginning to come out. Then, to "absorb" all traces of the evil, the egg is rolled all over the sick person. Next cleansing herbs are sprinkled on the person. Finally the egg is broken. Old rotten eggs are often used in this ceremony so that the broken egg, looking and smelling awful, can appropriately symbolize that the sickness has left the person and gone into the egg.

Magical Spells

Among the magic spells used by witches, perhaps the most fascinating were the flying ointments. Was it possible that witches really flew? If so, was it all due to a magical ointment?

There were many recipes for *flying ointment*. One, made from fairly common ingredients, is described in Thomas G. Aylesworth's *The Story of Witches*. It includes water parsnip, sweet flag, cinquefoil, bat's blood, deadly nightshade, and soot. All were mixed together and rubbed on the body. Other flying ointments included many different kinds of herbs and other ingredients, some common, some hard to obtain. Some called for such repulsive things as fat from babies. In most cases, at least some of the herbs used in the ointments were poisonous or affected the nervous system in unusual ways—causing tremors, hallucinations, dizziness, and rapid heart beat. One theory is that the effects of the ingredients in the ointments made people *think* that they had flown when in reality they had only experienced narcotic dreams.

While the supposed power of witches' charms are well-known to us, witches weren't the only ones to use magic. Even ordinary people used spells and charms—often purchased from a witch, often a combination of Christian and magical belief, and often used to get rid of a witch's influence.

Leonard Ashley reports that people around Lancashire, England, would say this charm *to protect their homes and family from harm*:

Sun, Moon, Mars, Mercury, Jupiter, Venus, Saturn, trine, sextile, dragon's head, dragon's tail, I charge ye all to gard this house from all evil spirits whatever, and gard it from all desorders, and from aney thing being taken wrangasly, and give this famaly good ealth and welth.

Many people hung strings of garlic around their home as a charm *to keep witches away*. Another anti-witch substance was common table salt. Tossed into a fire and burned, it was said to keep witches away from the home. In some countries, the head of a wolf was nailed to the door to prevent harm by witchcraft. A number of people tried a spell such as this Old English one:

Black-luggie, hammer-head,
Rowan-tree, and red thread,
Put the warlocks to their speed.

Another anti-witch charm, popular in the late sixteenth century according to Frances Wilkens, was this little poem:

Matthew, Mark, Luke, and John
Bless the bed that I lie on.
Four corners to my bed.
Five angels there lie spread,
Two at my head and two at my feet
And one at my heart my soul to keep.

Sometimes when someone was sick or was acting strangely, people didn't know if it was a natural condition or if the person was under a witch's spell. *To discover if a child was bewitched* a parent might put three small apples into a pan of water and put the pan under the child's bed. If the apples floated, the child was not bewitched; if they sank, the child was bewitched.

Sometimes those who believed in witches didn't realize until too late that an evil spell had been put on them. But there were certain ways *to counteract the effects of witchcraft*. One of the most popular was the witch bottle: The victim's urine and some of his or her hair or nail clippings were placed in a bottle along with other items such as nails, pins, or thorns. The bottle was corked. All doors and windows were closed and everyone sat about in silence. Then at midnight, the bottle was boiled on a fire. This would cause the witch to suffer great pain and she would beg to be let into the house. If the bottle exploded, it meant that the witch would die and her magic would be ended. But if the cork popped up, the witch would escape.

Spells To Get What You Want

Many cultures believed in the *magical use of knotted cords.* By using certain combinations of colors, certain numbers of threads, and certain numbers of knots at specific intervals, both good and bad magic could be performed. In some cases, it was a matter of *un*-tying the cords. Ancient Vikings, for example, believed they could control the sailing weather if they obtained a three-knot cord from a witch. If they untied one knot, they would raise a breeze; untying two would cause a strong wind; and untying all three would bring about a full-fledged storm.

At times, people still use cord magic *to make a desired thing happen.* One method is to obtain a long cord and tie forty knots at regular intervals. Then, each morning upon waking and just before falling asleep each night, hold the cord. At each knot, say aloud the thing you want to happen and visualize it as though it has already happened. Believers say that within a short time, the desired event should occur.

According to Leonard Ashley, an incense can be made which will help *improve the chances of success*. Combine the following ingredients: six parts sandalwood, two parts myrrh, one part patchouli leaf, one part orris root, two parts cinnamon, and eight parts frankincense. Add a dash of saltpeter and burn as you chant your desire.

Or, you can try *to put a spell on your rivals* and win by making them lose. In ancient Rome, it was possible to buy stone tablets with magical spells on them that would cause such a thing to happen. One tablet was found that was designed to prevent a rival's horses from winning a race. It was inscribed, "I summon you demon and hand over to you these horses to keep them and bind them so that they cannot move." Presumably, the person using the tablet would have to do something special with the tablet such as secreting it in the rival's horse equipment.

One thing people often use magic for is *to obtain love*. Witches might give the love-seeker a special charm or they might give them something to bewitch the object of their love. William Butler Yeats, the Irish poet, reported that love potions could be made by drying and then grinding into powder a black cat's liver. If the powder was mixed with tea and poured from a black teapot, he said, it would be a sure thing.

Here are three "love charm" traditions reported by Leonard Ashley: In Malaysia, the sand from the footprint of the beloved is fried to make him or her itch with desire. Arabs write special characters in oil on the palm of their hand, then rub the hand on their own face when the object of their love is near. Some Americans count the seeds of an apple while reciting this poem:

> One I love, two I love, three I love, I say.
> Four I love with all my heart.
> Five I'll cast away.
> Six he loves, seven she loves,
> Eight they both love.
> Nine he comes, ten he tarries,
> Eleven he courts, twelve he marries.

The number of seeds the apple has tells the future of the counter's relationship with the person he or she desires.

Putting spells on another person is done in many cultures with the help of an image of the person. Witches were known to make figures out of wax, clay, straw, or other substances. Often they dressed the figure in scraps from the object-person's own clothing, sometimes with pieces of the object-person's hair or some nail clippings. Most users of images seem to think that the spell becomes more powerful if something from the object-person can be obtained and used.

Poet Erica Jong, in her book *Witches*, described a love ritual, "guaranteeing" eternal love, that involves using an image of the beloved. She says this ritual is most effective when performed on a Friday, the day sacred to Venus and Freya, goddesses of love.

On a piece of paper—if possible, one your love-object has touched—draw a pattern for a doll thirteen inches high. Lay this pattern on two pieces of old bedsheet and cut them out, all the time thinking of your beloved. Sew the two pieces of sheet together, leaving an opening at the top for stuffing. Stuff the doll with sweet-smelling herbs and sew the opening closed. Make another doll to represent you. Decorate the dolls to represent your beloved and yourself: Paint or embroider symbols of the two of you on the dolls—for example, a football if he likes to play that game, a camera if photography is your favorite hobby, and so on. If you have anything from your beloved such as a piece of hair or a souvenir movie ticket, put this in the stuffing or sew it on the outside of the doll. You can also make the features and clothing resemble those of your beloved and yourself.

Now, cut several red ribbons in lengths that are multiples of seven inches (fourteen inches, twenty-one, etc.). Holding the dolls in your hands, think about the two of you intertwined forever in love. Bring the two dolls together face to face, and bind them with the red ribbons. Finally, wrap the dolls in a piece of cloth and hide them in a safe place.

Jong says to repeat this ritual the following two Fridays, if necessary.

Do Spells and Charms Work?

Will such spells work? Some people believe they do; others believe they are nonsense. Some believe that there may be some power in such things but that it is dangerous power, even when used to do good; fooling around with magic, they say, may invite Satan into our world. Many modern-day witches believe that spells and charms are truly magic; others say that it is simply strong belief and will power that make them work. Skeptics argue that any charms that "work" are really only coincidence. What do you think?

Index

Illustration Credits

Amy Johnson, pp. 10, 17, 20, 28, 32, 37, 48, 51, 60, 66, 72, 73, 78, 82, 84, 94, 96, 98.
Mary Evans Picture Library, pp. 14, 22, 26, 53, 74, 90, 93.
Courtesy of Dover Publications, from *Picture Book of Devils, Demons and Witchcraft* by Ernst and Johanna Lehner, pp. 25, 34, 35, 50, 58, 59.
Picture Collection, The Branch Libraries, The New York Public Library, pp. 31, 38, 42, 46, 56, 64.
Wide World Photos, pp. 40, 80.
Courtesy of the Library of Congress, p. 45.
Courtesy of McGraw-Hill Book Company, from *The Story of Witches* by Thomas G. Aylesworth, p. 52.
Ann Ronan Picture Library, pp. 68, 86, 88, 89.
From *Witches* by Erica Jong. Illustrations © 1981 by Harry N. Abrams, pp. 70, 101.

About the Author

When she was six years old, Bryna Stevens wrote a poem that was published in the school newspaper. That was the start of her career as a writer. Being fascinated by history, Bryna frequently writes nonfiction. She says that she finds things that actually happened far more interesting than anything a writer could imagine.

Among Bryna's books are *Ben Franklin's Glass Armonica* and *George Handel and the Famous Sword Swallower of Halle*. Her book *Deborah Sampson Goes to War* won an award from the Virginia Library Association.

Bryna attended Music and Art High School in New York City. She taught music in public schools for several years and presently teaches piano privately, combining careers in music and writing. She lives in San Francisco.